PRACTICING ROMAN NUMERALS

MATH BOOK 6TH GRADE

Children's Math Books

Speedy Publishing LLC
40 E. Main St. #1156
Newark, DE 19711
www.speedypublishing.com

Let's Begin with Roman Numerals

ONE

TWO

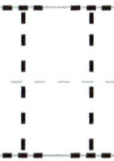

THREE

V - I = ?

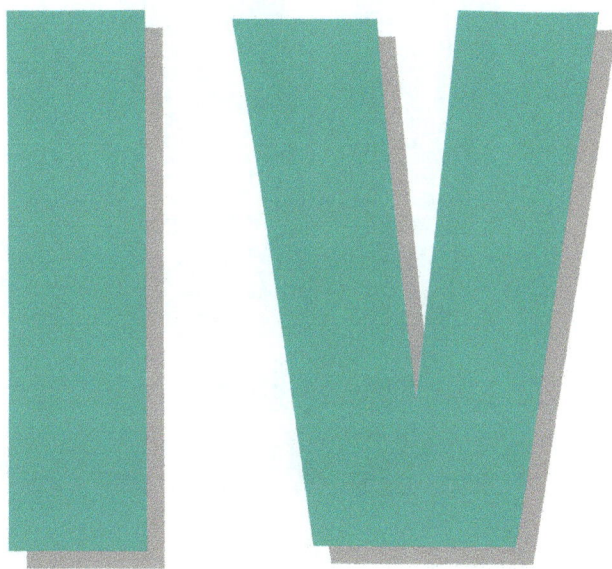

IV
FOUR

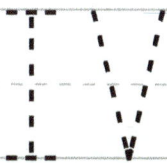

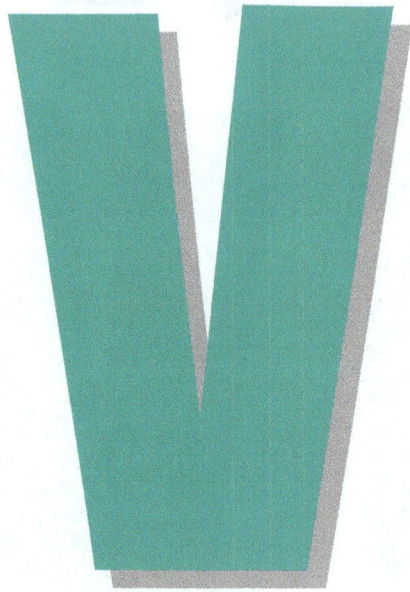

FIVE

VI

SIX

V I

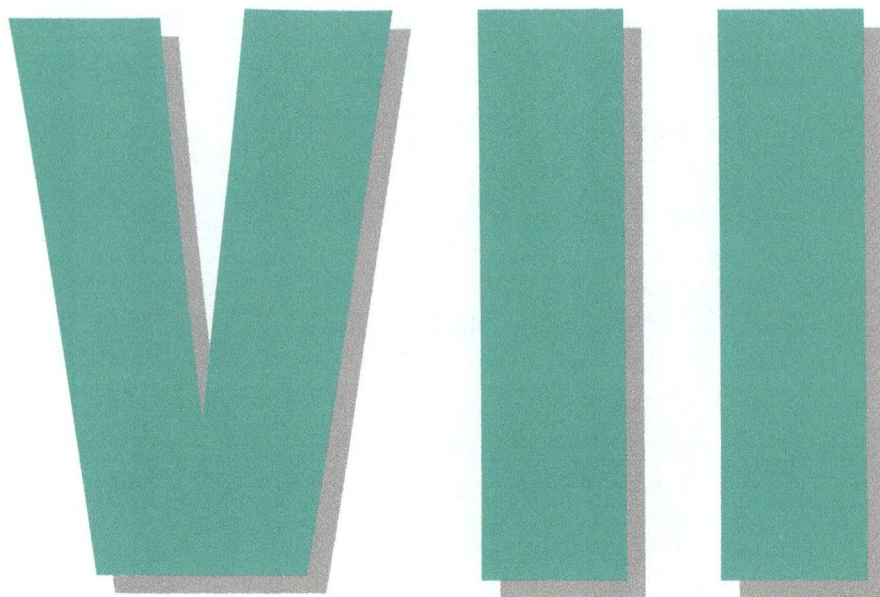

SEVEN

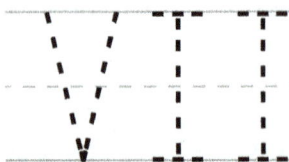

VIII

EIGHT

V I I I

X - 1 = ?

IX

NINE

IX

TEN

XI

ELEVEN

XI

XII

TWELVE

XII

XIII

THIRTEEN

XIII

XV - I = ?

XIV

FOURTEEN

XIV

XV

FIFTEEN

xv

XVI

SIXTEEN

XVI

XVII

SEVENTEEN

X V I I

XVIII

EIGHTEEN

XVIII

XX - 1 = ?

XIX
NINETEEN

XIX

XX

TWENTY

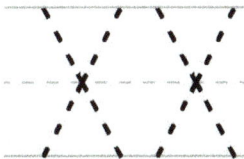

XXI

TWENTY-ONE

XXI

XXII

TWENTY-TWO

XXII

XXIII

TWENTY-THREE

XXIII

XXV - I = ?

XXIV
TWENTY-FOUR

XXIV

XXV

TWENTY-FIVE

X X V

XXVI

TWENTY-SIX

XXVI

XXVII

TWENTY-SEVEN

XXVII

XXVIII

TWENTY-EIGHT

XXVIII

XXX - I = ?

XXIX

TWENTY-NINE

XXIX

XXX

THIRTY

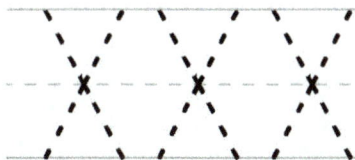

XXXI

THIRTY-ONE

XXXI

XXXII

THIRTY-TWO

XXXII

L - X = ?

XL
FORTY

XL

FIFTY

LX

SIXTY

LXX

SEVENTY

L X X

LXXX

EIGHTY

L X X X

XC

NINETY

xc

C

ONE HUNDRED

CC

TWO HUNDRED

CC

CCC

THREE HUNDRED

ccc

D - C = ?

CD

FOUR HUNDRED

CD

D

FIVE HUNDRED

D

DC

SIX HUNDRED

DC

DCC

SEVEN HUNDRED

DCC

DCCC

EIGHT HUNDRED

DCCC

M - C = ?

CM

NINE HUNDRED

CM

M

ONE THOUSAND

M

Let's Do Some Maths with Roman Numerals

1. II + II = ?

2. IV + I = ?

3. V + III = ?

4. VII - V = ?

5. IV + IX = ?

6. X + VI = ?

7 $XX + X = $

8 $VI - I = $

9 $XV - V = $

10 VI + XV =

11 XI + X =

12 I - I =

13. III + III =

14. VI − IV =

15. VIII + X =

16 XIV - I =

17 XI + X =

18 VI + II =

19 VI + V =

20 X - II =

21 V + XX =

Answers

1. IV
2. V
3. VIII
4. II
5. XIII
6. XVI
7. XXX
8. V
9. X
10. XXI
11. XXI
12. O
13. VI
14. II
15. XVIII
16. XIII
17. XXI
18. XXV
19. XI
20. VIII
21. VIII

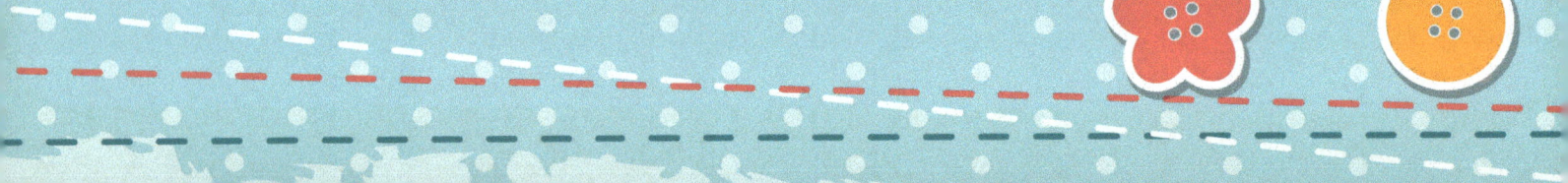

Visit

BABY PROFESSOR
EDUCATION KIDS

www.BabyProfessorBooks.com

to download Free Baby Professor eBooks
and view our catalog of new and exciting
Children's Books

Milton Keynes UK
Ingram Content Group UK Ltd.
UKHW051136030924
447802UK00003B/225